Salamander, Frog, and Polliwog

For my friends at St. Christopher School
in Rocky River, Ohio

                                                        —B.P.C.

To Loulou and Gilles, my godparents

                                                        —M.G.

Amphibian:
an animal with
a backbone that
has no feathers,
fur, hair, scales,
or claws on
its body

Salamander, Frog, and Polliwog

What Is an Amphibian?

by Brian P. Cleary

illustrations by Martin Goneau

M Millbrook Press • Minneapolis

a lake or stream, or on dry land,
and most will have smooth skin.

All of them have backbones,
and they have no scales or fur.

Plus, they're all cold-blooded, which affects their temperature.

Unlike you or me, they have their body temp transformed

by what's in their environment:

from cool . . .

to hot . . .

to warm.

Amphibians are born from eggs that don't have any shell.

Instead, the eggs are made of something gooey, like a gel.

When most are born,
they breathe through gills
beneath the water, and

as they get older, they'll grow lungs and spend more time on land.

Some have solid-colored skin,

while some
have dots

or stripes.

And all around the world,
there are a host
of different types.

Toads are in this class, or group.
The same is true of frogs.

At birth, they're both called tadpoles or sometimes polliwogs.

The kids don't look like grown-ups
(not even just a "tad")

18 days

2 days

first steps

when they've first hatched, but over time, they'll look like Mom and Dad.

One type of **amphibian** looks like a snake or worm.

In water, mud, or dirt, it's known
to slither, swim, and squirm.

These legless creatures burrow,
with a head that's blunt and strong,

and range from just your finger's length

to nearly five feet long!

Salamanders tend to like the damp and dark to thrive.

Their front feet mainly have four toes. Their back feet? Mostly five.

Sometimes one will wave its tail
when enemies are near

and then escape just as it drops—
detaching at the rear!

Amphibians are awesome.
They've survived throughout the ages.

So, what is an amphibian? Do you know?

An animal is an amphibian if...
· it has a backbone (it is a vertebrate) and has no feathers, fur, hair, scales, or claws

In addition, all amphibians...
· are cold-blooded. That means they cannot make their own body heat. Their bodies are the same temperature as their surroundings.

And most amphibians...
· live underwater and breathe with gills while young and live on land and breathe with lungs as adults;
· are born from eggs;
· have smooth skin.

31

For more facts that are "ribbiting," just look in these last pages!

So, what is an **amphibian**?
Do you know?

An animal is an amphibian if...
- it has a backbone (it is a vertebrate) and has no feathers, fur, hair, scales, or claws.

In addition, all amphibians...

- are cold-blooded. That means they cannot make their own body heat. Their bodies are the same temperature as their surroundings.

And most amphibians...

- live underwater and breathe with gills while young and live on land and breathe with lungs as adults;
- are born from eggs;
- have smooth skin.

Find activities, games, and more at
www.brianpcleary.com

ABOUT THE AUTHOR & ILLUSTRATOR

BRIAN P. CLEARY is the author of the Words Are CATegorical®, Math Is CATegorical®, Adventures in Memory™, Sounds Like Reading®, and Food Is CATegorical™ series, as well as several picture books and poetry books. He lives in Cleveland, Ohio.

MARTIN GONEAU is the illustrator of the Food Is CATegorical™ series. He lives in Trois-Rivières, Québec.

LERNER e SOURCE™

Expand learning beyond this printed book. Download free, complementary educational resources for this book from our website, www.lernersource.com.

Millbrook Press
A division of Lerner Publishing Group, Inc.
241 First Avenue North
Minneapolis, MN 55401 U.S.A.

Website address: www.lernerbooks.com

Toad Skin Background: © Xunbin Pan/Dreamstime.com.

Main body text set in Chauncy Decaf Medium 35/44. Typeface provided by the Chank Company.

Library of Congress Cataloging-in-Publication Data

Cleary, Brian P., 1959–
    Salamander, frog, and polliwog : what is an amphibian? / by Brian P. Cleary ; illustrated by Martin Goneau.
      p.   cm. — (Animal groups are CATegorical)
    ISBN 978-0-7613-6209-8 (lib. bdg. : alk. paper)
    1. Amphibians—Juvenile literature. I. Goneau, Martin, ill. II. Title.
  QL644.2.C587 2013
  597.8—dc23   2011050202

Manufactured in the United States of America
1 – DP – 7/15/2012